MW01624041

Passing Reflections

Volume 2

The Journey Through Grief

Kristen Spexarth

Printed in the United States of America.

Visit the book's site at www.passingreflections.com

For information, visit us at Big Think Media, Inc., www.bigthinkmedia.com, or contact us at info@bigthinkmedia.com

ISBN-978-0-9788108-3-2

For My Son Arlen

with deep love

and for all those
who have shared this journey with me

Life is so beautiful, in its
triumphs and tragedies.
Everywhere I look I see it now.
There is beauty even in fear
and pain, but visible only to
those deeply submerged in it.

- Colby Spexarth

Table of Contents

Acknowledgments

There are many stages in the development of a book, from the first need to pen notes on paper to the final tangible product, resting comfortably in your hands. Bringing this work to completion has brought with it a monumental process of growth for me. Fraught with seeming obstructions at times, still I was compelled to move it forward by an urgency coming from within. Noticing this process I began to discern that every seeming obstacle was in fact a gift, making space for gathering energy and clarity about my intentions.

Throughout these eight years of noticing, whenever I felt "…without a clue as to how or where I should go from here…" (from "Noticing – Day 121," Vol. 1) people have appeared, offering their considerable skills and encouragement—dear friends whose generosity and love have made this book possible. For all of you, near and far, my sincere thanks.

Principal among these helpers has been my agent, Arushi Sinha, whose work has made this book a reality. Her bountiful energy, wide-ranging talents and unflagging support continue to be an inspiration. Larry Wight created **www.passingreflections.com**, a website whereby I could reach countless people suffering loss. Susan Lebow, whose understanding of my work buoyed me up many a time, helped with editing. Richard Dean co-produced with Susan a CD of Volume 1, providing access to the poems through the spoken word. Esther Helfgott, mentor and friend to numerous poets in the Northwest, was an inspiration with her workshops and reading series, It's About Time.

In addition, I want to thank Michelle Duncan, Judy Jacob, Jean and Terry Keller, Melinda Moore, Vincent de Rosa, Jude Rozhon, and Paris Yates, whose belief in this work helped me persevere. To my extended family members who have been there with love and support throughout, thank you.

For Colby, gone before, forever will you live in my heart. And for Arlen, whose love and understanding transcended the difficulties we have encountered along the way, my love and gratitude. May your "journey through" always be graced by the knowing that comes from within, as well as the love and support of those around you.

Introduction

This book of poems, in journal form, brings to completion a body of work that spans the two-year period after I lost my eldest son, Colby, to suicide. He was twenty-two. Not knowing at the start where the journey would lead, it is now clear to me; this work is an entity unto itself with a life of its own. It came to me much like a child comes to any mother, with a tenderness, forcefulness and urgency characteristic of all life.

Compounding the trauma that precipitated *Passing Reflections* was the felling of the Twin Towers in New York City and shortly thereafter the brutal murder of a dear friend. It seemed that just as my life began to stabilize, events threw me back into a state of shock and deep grief. Finding no solid ground, writing became a tether keeping me from drifting away.

Grieving is hard but important work. Many of us want the pain of loss to just go away. Fearing we'll bc overwhelmed by our feelings, we seek any means of distraction, hoping thereby to avoid our discomfort. But pushing pain away does not bring release and with the next impact, from even small losses, we find the difficulty compounded by having long refused our grief work.

The deaths of my son and my friend created trauma so severe it broke me open, beyond fear, past all resistance to delving deeply into what I was experiencing. Strange as it may seem, in this opening

I count myself lucky. While not an easy journey, I was compelled to explore my new world for, "… The strangest part is, this version of real is more vital and essential than any I have ever lived and looking around it is clear to me, I am surrounded by the virtual." (from Vol. 1, "Virtual Reality")

Sensitized to an alarming degree, when people approached me with fear, as they often did, it felt like a physical assault. Some well-intentioned words struck so hard my body would recoil, seeking shelter. Writing then became a place of respite and reflection, simply noticing what IS.

Once seeming contradictions were suddenly resolved when viewed from my new vantage; the scales were broken and this world of dual with its pairs of opposites—good/bad, right/wrong, loss/gain, pleasure/pain—were revealed, a wholeness. I felt at peace with the paradoxical nature of things and then, falling back into notions of what I longed for or what I feared or how things "should be," I could feel my body tighten. When I managed to simply sit with my feelings, not attaching any storylines, the sensations though uncomfortable, became manageable.

Back and forth I struggled until learning to stay with the sensations and new awareness accompanying loss, breathing into them, noticing everything, relaxing when my body tightened around an idea or my breath caught in my throat. In this laborsome way I discovered that leaning into, rather than away from what IS, is key to finding release from pain—a paradox. With this dawning I have been finding my way through the labyrinth, birthing myself in a world larger and more beautiful than I ever imagined, whether waking or sleeping.

Pain softens with time but it does not "go away." Just like all the events of a lifetime, happy or sad, they remain part of us. To find healing, our task is to learn how to weave all of life's events into the fabric of our being in a manageable way. Opened by loss I was transformed from the small, separate creature I once imagined myself to be, into a wholeness that IS, suffused with joy. My need to self-protect dissolved in a knowing that there is nothing "other," at which point instead of consuming judgments setting me apart, I found in my heart compassion, and writing became a reaching out, to lend a hand to others suffering loss.

Recovering from trauma requires one's attention. To find release from the pain of loss one has to go the distance and do the hard work of discovery, but I believe there is no more important work, nothing of greater consequence. My former life and what once seemed "real" to me ended with my son's traumatic death—a tragedy of immense proportions that set in motion a gift of awareness, helping me not only survive but grow. As Colby said,

Life is so beautiful, in its
triumphs and tragedies.
Everywhere I look I see it now.
There is beauty even in fear
and pain, but visible only to
those deeply submerged in it.

I offer these poems to you, to read aloud, in the hope they will comfort you on your own journey of discovery.

May it be of benefit.

Kristen Spexarth

October 18, 2008
Seattle, Washington

Passing Reflections

Volume 2

The Journey Through Grief

October
2001

The Web

We spoke of those gossamer unseen links
that keep us anchored in this place
each one a strand of the web that is us
eternal spider spinning.

Losing love we are cut loose
web torn and blowing on the breeze
the fabric of days ripped beyond belief
as we try to cope with loss.

Attempts to re-weave links to place
emerge from where I left them last
and puzzle me exceedingly,
if energy threads are indeed the source

how do we get so tangled in things?
Boundlessness beyond thinking and dreaming
with strength eclipsing time and space,
no matter which way my body turns

strings of relatedness strummed at each step
sing the song of arriving
—a humming connectivity
deeper than I've ever dreamed
whether waking or sleeping.

October 8, 2001
Seattle

Disconnected

Late start, mid-week,
disconnected energy
found my usual parking space
taken.

Rearranging patterns,
checking schedule,
headed for a different bus
traversing rainy hypotenuse

smelling a tropical express
coming from the dryer's vent
hard working
at the Laundromat.

Through underpass
the leaves were dry
and scuffling, skittered
this way and that.

Foliage in trees is all aglow,
a vibrancy larger than color
luminescence shimmering,
making ready to go,

the gray above somber
only if I make it so,
quieting, softening,
enhancing every hue and tint,

green merging with cement,
a glowing sheen on wetness
registering every vertical element
as shadow.

Rolling along I see leaves
strewn on road and path
like petals for an emperor
or empress,

who must be all of us
for here we stand
having debarked the bus
in splashes

of yellow exuberance
and crimson and orange
leaves aflame as they lie
soaking wet on pavement.

A week ago the wind came up
and took a tree or two
as swirling leaves
and flocks of birds,

each group registering heightened senses,
excitement charged, swooped and dove
riding huge energies as one,
clustering, expanding then retracting,

subtle connectivity of part to whole
played out with deft dexterity
wing tip to wing tip
and petiole to petiole

twisting and soaring in the firmament
every bit of it in movement
echoing a heartbeat racing
anticipating the coming event.

October 25, 2001
Seattle

Cozy Cats

The trees are ablaze in October's bliss
colors running riotous,

rain pounding all night long,
cats longing for dirt under paw

sit front porch pondering the likelihood
of its stopping anytime soon.

Like a jeweled curtain the drops form a veil
draped from the overhanging roof.

Looking out my window
at this dazzling scene,
Buddha sitting amidst fallen leaves

and pods suspended from dry stalks, brittle,
making ready to cast their seed

next to the rock where the cats once basked
warming in sun's radiant heat

I feel at peace and grateful
for a space in time so beautiful.

October 27, 2001
Seattle

Suspended Animation

Rain is pouring down outside
street gutters, waves
in rapid succession
surging toward leaf-stoppered drains

pelting raindrops on bus-top roof
I sit and contemplate where I am
unable, lately
to discern certain subtleties.

Suspended animation
seems the best I can do
working and trying to live a life
yet not really present inside it

the most lucid moments come as I sit
the rest of time feigning, a reflexive shutter
opening then closing so rapidly
few can detect

while I seem to be moving
it's not true.
I am a cartoon, inert, still-life creation
utterly unable to engage.

A stillness has descended,
a stopping of activity
awaiting a key to the mystery—
how to resolve my deep grief.

Neither does it leave
nor do thoughts of you

and I feel life suspended
around me.

Days come and go
and I move along
but my heart
is no longer in it.

Like a nursing home resident
worrying her porridge,
lifting spoon, missing mouth,
staring vacantly,

I seem to have
checked out of my body
leaving behind
a facsimile.

Some are fooled by this hobbled pretense,
nodding and waving greetings
but there are those so provoked
by my absence

they angrily try to hammer me back,
a violence so strange in its intensity
I try to reconnect
with little real success.

October 30, 2001
Seattle

Union News

The picture showed a woman's face
from Cambodia in the 80s it said
and my mind's eye, scanning memory banks
trying to imagine her journey,
flashed on unimaginable scenes
as if I was viewing a movie.

She looked younger than I,
drawn to read by happenstance
noting kindness written in her glance,
"Died of a heart attack at work," it read
leaving two young children in her stead and I
could not turn the page
seeing her there
smiling at me
seeming so near and yet…

So hard to lose a child, I know,
the meaning of life gone out of existence
passing days measured in coffee dregs
noting leaves lit by sun and breeze
with a radiance deeper than matter.
Still, to be taken from your children's youth
seemed to me even worse.

She reached out and touched me
where I stood,
kitchen table, Sunday morning,
reading the union news.

October 30, 2001
Seattle

November 2001

Seattle Sentinel

A vacancy fills the sky
near the big leaf maple "Seattle Sentinel."
Its sibling we took down weeks ago
fallen victim to a cataclysmic invasion
all rotting and weakened by fungus
swiftly ending this mighty neighbor.
Out on my rounds
scanning sky's perimeter
I can't help but pause at the hole
standing gaping where once the tree stood
and wonder if others will notice this?
Dynamic forces pulling at that spot
mourning and mending the cavity.

November 2, 2001
Walker Ames Estate

Day 308

This sound of waves brings me cheer
and sea smell, floating past on gentle breeze,
the sun is here and warming so
I touch hand to sand and feel the heat
only on the west facing shelf
cut by last tide's leaving.
Topside is cool and moist below thin crust
November coming fast upon us
hardly a barefoot on the beach
just a couple of wetsuit enthusiasts
and children down the way
up to shorts-clad thighs
splashing, in youthful exuberance.
Marina full of sticks has gone deciduous
and the rolling slope to the east is a glowing,
golden froth of big leaf maple leaves
like curling wave's majestic crest
foaming sunset over top.
Here comes one blissful, barefooted child
way behind her parents
all winter coat draped and zippered up tight
as she strolls the waves softly humming
clad in pink,
short-sleeved shirt with jeans rolled up.
Ah youth, clothes can't contain it
as the waves, in honor, nestle her toes
gently loving her abandon.
Here comes a father with child riding high,
blue skull-cap and silent regal gaze

as a seagull bobs like a cork over waves
just before they crest,
rolling in from the west
and laying down, here, at my feet.
The train behind echoes past
reminding me of your last visit
and words you shared to ease my sadness
for a friend lost to the tracks
the gist of which said we do what we must
and the lingering, clinging,
should be put to rest.
At the time I thought, "Yes,
that's wisdom's reply,"
but sitting here thoughts swirl in my head
bumping up against each other
switching yard full
and no one to guide them.
I'll let the breeze take them
where it will, sitting here still and empty
unburdened by a mind's meandering
blending with the world I feel
gently cradling my being.

November 3, 2001
Shilshole

Fall Color

When they don their fall finery
my feet stop mid-step
and stand
soaking in a presence so grand
it seems the first time
ever witnessed.
When did I ever take the chance
to notice them, individuals?
Now arrayed in earth's change
I cannot work past
lost in my everyday
somnambulistic trance.

They grab me by my shoulders
and give me a shake
dusting off my incredulity
that life could be so.
Some, all drama, glowing orange and red,
knit together with browns and greens
to weave a radiant tapestry
alive with luminescent threads
spun of down still tethered
to my deepest self
and there is no other place I need be.

November 3, 2001
Seattle

The Chicken and The Egg

Through visions long ago
I learned reverence
for those who came before,
the pavers of paths
I would have to tread.

Now he who came after
has joined the rest
and the order of existence
that I thought I knew
has been shattered,

rendered
upside down and backwards
as I try to comprehend
the chicken
and the egg.

Slowly
and with gentle persistence
glimmers of wisdom shine on me
and now I see
from a certain point of view

it doesn't matter.
No chicken,
no egg
and all that is left is, simply,
reverence.

November 3, 2001
Seattle

Troubled

Deeply troubled, it's true,
I can feel a wringing of hands
wondering
if needed help is getting through.
But so many do not fit the mold.

Look!
See them falling
between cracks I'm inclined
to slip right by, too, puddling
with the misfits around me.

I bear no judgment in this.
As awkward
and painful as my truth might be
it's a simple fact
that finding comfort

with those who can feel
is vastly more healing
than the shaving of corners
off square-ish pegs
in order to fit in holes round-ish.

This pressure to be
just like I was
instead of who I am
may indeed not
be coming from you

but all distractions from what is,
these figments of my recent past,
are baggage
dragging heavily,
time now to open to the real.

November 9, 2001
Seattle

Whiplash

I will grow old and you will not.

How many the times I've thought
with comfort
of two old friends navigating
and gallivanting through our
elder years, together
if none the wiser.

Always a beauty, held erect
yet how many could suspect
the pain that made you so?
The dignity of your deep strength
in spite of setbacks, many
as you searched for the thread
of love and meaning that could bind
your wounds.

And this further wounding
act of taking, and leaving
took from those who loved you,
everything.
How could this be true?
I am thrown back, whiplash
in my grieving
to that beginning absent of reason
flailing, searching for solid ground
that is cruelly not forthcoming.

And your family who number many
so deep in shock there could be no fathoming
the depth of loss still coming,

bearing up, bearing up
brave-hearted every one of them
gathering blood lines under roof
readying, planning
phalanx against the storm
impending.

November 11, 2001
Seattle

Mudra

Morris Graves said it in paint,
gloved expressions floating
still,
absent of a person to fill
empty
and mirrored here on pavement
in a single abandoned glove

yet strangely animate
holding the pattern of he who wore it
ever seeking that which eludes
reminding me of that deep yearning
prodding, driving,
searching for a clue

and seeking, too, I asked the man
residing on street corner
who'd made an offering to the world—
six-bit answers to any query,
"Please tell me
the meaning of life."

He prattled on for quite a while
most of it pure gibberish
but in between sounds as he scanned the sky
for words to fill the vacuum
I could feel him struggling and reaching,
feel the longing for connection

and somehow in that vacancy
of thirsting, pure and simple
he answered the question that I'd posed
not with his words but in the space that lives,
the void between the lines,
as he strained to fill the unfillable.

November 16, 2001
Seattle

At Sea in Eastern Washington

Rolling along
riding freeway swells and dips
passing solitary farms
like distant sailing ships
blinking in and out of view
hidden by rolling waves of wheat
pitching and heaving in the night,
I see a blanketing gray, vaporous sheet
over chasm torn by the mighty Columbia
cresting, curling, splashing over ridge top
as red and white streams of light
glowing ribbons in a sea of black
wind toward a narrowing infinity.
Moon over shoulder is now a high quarter
beaming through fuzzy, gray coverlet
and dusk's last glimmer on distant horizon
is melting into night.
Desert low-riding
shoulder artemisia
become beach flora through the dark
rooted in sandy, white volcanic ash
as black gold of buried humic treasure
nurtures a sea of grass.
Roiling volcanic layers emerge
from where the road's wake cuts
showing waves of earth's changing face
while nearby tug of car-to-car
rides an endless magnetic subtlety
suspended across an ocean of time

and cedars stand like bull kelp swaying
in the turbulent ocean of sky.
An ocean of feelings here in my heart
is spilling from my eyes
as I stand on the bottom of
life's greatest depths
pondering the distance between life and death
land surfing soils worked by rain and wind
just like the sea uses sand.
In the darkness wheat sways
like ocean-floor eelgrass,
blackened strands
layered against a blackened sky,
tumbling in a swirling torrent
and I,
sailing toward a distant shore
am at sea in the depths of my mind.

November 20, 2001
I-90 East

Obituary

Our tendency is
to lay down the events
attempting to display
a lifetime's contents
on spreadsheet, in brackets
as if we understood.

Our tendency is
to wrap things up
as if somehow done and finished
noting details gathered
where paths intersected
where we were for a moment
connected.

Witness to this ritual
I now see more clearly
the essence, lacking substance
cannot be reconstructed.

Physicists postulate alternate realities
and perhaps this holds some truth
for every time we share time and space
our deeply layered universe
can be seen for an instant
a crossroads of different dimensions
as many as there are people.

But standing on the threshold
of Death's bitter taking, here,

at the gate of Rashomon's wisdom
each of us cloaked in disparate visions
we live in dimensions separate,
even distant,

like parallel ports
shunting massive amounts
of discretely packaged ingredients
and blind to so much and so many
our longing for connection
ephemeral it seems
too often lived solely in dream
as we weave single strands
through life's infinite unfoldings.

Your time with me
though spanning a lifetime
was more butterfly, alighting then leaving,
the stuff of friendship bridging the gaps
as we went about raising our families.
But I remember the pain, a perennial theme
arising, I guessed, from an absence felt
as you longed for the bliss of a deeper union
once shared with the partner Death took.

So many times an ear for you
I came to know the heartbreak—
to have once tasted the nectar of bliss
the question remained: how to continue
absent of that communing?

And how could there be blame in this,
fed by a culture that feeds the myth—
that there is only one true happiness,
we struggle through days to gain
understanding
why it seems so hard to find it.

The end of line news printed wishful claim
that you were living a life
of mythic completion
came as a further shock to me,
reeling from the blow of your brutal leaving,
sheltering words for those left in your wake
which to me seemed cruel in light of the truth,
an affect of social boilerplate.

But you are gone. What harm can it do
if some need to think a lie, true?
My heart and mind recoil from this
wishing you not only greater fulfillment
but an honoring of your deepest truth.

As days go by I am beginning to see,
stuck to the notion that we own validity
is simply clinging to illusion
and anger over words said by a family
grieving and grasping after threads
holds a mirror not to truth but to frustration
at our helplessness in the face of Death.

And I find that while searching for
fantasy mates

we miss the ones here, at Rashomon's gate,
each of us partners in this cosmic unfolding
life's fabric, a weaving of strands, mated
by our simply sharing this time-space web.

And as each of us weaves our version of truth
how can we judge others' absence of insight
when we stand as one at the gates
with no more clue to the meaning of events
than we had at the start of our journey?

While I am certain you have forgiven us,
struggling in your absence,
they with words that naught was amiss
and me, grief rendered sudden pugilist,
standing at the gate of your departure
the choices we face emerge from the mist—
is this portal a means to illuminate
or an illusion propping bolster?

November 21, 2001
Sandpoint, Idaho

Thanksgiving Dinner

Beautiful turkey and all the trimmings
she sat apart, surrounded by loved ones.
One could tell by looking with
eyes that can see
she'd been hard hit—gaping hole
in her chest standing vacant.

They seemed to make as if
nothing was different
and she wondered how they did it.
"Let's drink a toast to life!" said one,
and she added, "And to death,"
pondering how to blend
with life's giddy avoidance

without going completely numb.
"Let it go, let it go," her mind murmured,
"there is nothing you can do,"
remembering she'd almost made it back,
almost able to engage anew when further loss

hurled her back to pain
and back to the questioning.
She'd asked everyone she knew,
even some she didn't
but none could give an answer's semblance
just annoyingly facile platitudes.

Sitting there poised on the edge of the brink
and grasping for an inkling of the truth

without speaking a word
they could all hear her pain
though no one knew what to do.
From that space a clamor arose

as ripples of energy coursed through the room
out to the stars and maybe further,
crying out for wisdom.
The reply that came was a softening
as those nearby reached out to her
with a gift of such resilient strength
—their love

and an offering to hold her close
while respecting her space in grief
and gradually there came a calming, settling
as she joined them in that place,
riding the tide of silence.

November 22, 2001
Sandpoint, Idaho

December 2001

Commuters

Something is going on under the dock.
Small black birds are winging in
from the north
toward the ferryboat ramp

and as they fly above the deck
they tumble and swoop
like party confetti,
twisting and turning

and catching the light
till the last possible moment
they pull up tight,
squeezing in amidst the pilings.

I've been here only a minute or two
and as I've been observing
several hundred birds have tucked
themselves in,
into a forest primeval.

This extraordinary migration
may simply be a commuter occasion
finished from a hard day's work
and heading home again.

December 5, 2001
Edmonds Landing

Bus Stop

Funny thing this morning
walking up the street
backpack slung on my right shoulder
swinging, I looked up
searching for the moon and saw

a cloud-like wisp of cotton fluff
floating, suspended in an ebony sea
then suddenly the image changed
and instead of a cloud
there was the moon!

The sky was cloaked in a thick, dark shroud
and through a small portal moonlight beamed.
As the clouds moved across
the light glimmered and faded
obscured by dense cover I'd taken for open,

seeing in reverse
thinking moonlight a cloud
a photo negative, turned upside down
and I felt my mind do a double-take flip
ever searching for the truth.

December 7, 2001
Lake City Bus Stop

Anger

Sitting at meeting
hearing other processes
other prose from other disasters
I kept asking if they'd punched in the nose
those thoughtless, inept, selfish clods
who inevitably step on sorrow's toes.
Twice I asked and twice came the answer, "no"
from those so broken and new to grieving
they could barely address my
cloddish intrusion.

I could never be angry with you.
Having watched you suffer and
realizing your answer
was the best that you could do
my grief limped along unconnected to anger.
Now I simply want to scream,
"Don't mess with me
—can't you see I'm broken!"
but the world keeps plowing
roughshod through
unperturbed by my tenuous condition.

At long last having found my anger,
now what do I do?
Discomfort acute with energies misfit
I cast about in fury
needing to ground like a lightning bolt
on any nearby object

but venting brings no real relief
and only makes me sadder
for in its wake the swath of destruction
is growing ever wider.

I'm going to have to sit with this
uncomfortable, difficult feeling
without attaching any blame
without needing any answer
just this feeling, that's all I know is true
and if I can sit and be present to
the hunger and hurting and needing
breathing them in and breathing out a healing
there may be hope for me.

December 10, 2001
Seattle

Layers of Significance

The layers of my existence keep piling on
and at present I seem to be the path
of least resistance.
My teachers say things aren't what they seem,
attachment the real source of pain
and life's struggle mostly misplaced attention
but the wounding I feel certainly seems
to be real
as I stumble and trip over everything.
Tattered and torn and struggling again
this time the cycles of grateful renewal,
that biological process we are visited with
emptiness, confusion, anger, pain
are cycling so fast I can't take a step
without lashing out at somebody.
Finding blame aplenty as if venting
could mend
when it only destroys my sanity,
the metaphors of "plus" and "minus"
and all they bring into being
seeming so guilefully real at the start
simply mirror this beginner's bumbling.
Perhaps anger serves to dislodge
useless patterns
getting so blown away we can then start again
but the end-run blame-game adds fuel
to a flame
that is burning me inside out.

Like compost's chemistry
it's hidden from view
and the antsy, jittery careening are proof
I've relinquished the wheel
to a child or an animal
that knows no better than to run from pain
believing the source of it real.
Think I'm getting the message this time
accelerated process abusing mind and body
for I see now anger is like any fix—
another trap to fall into.
Out of control and speeding rapidly
into red lights run and relations traumatic
it's time to rein in my brokenness
to find a quiet place to sit
and seek wise counsel for guidance
for nothing about venting or avoidance
is going to help me heal.
At this point of so much lost
I see there is nothing to win
but mastery over wild horses within
who are driving me to distraction.

December 10, 2001
Seattle

The Stream

The stream running through the parking lot
was four feet wide
and growing.
A torrent pouring down
had birds mostly on the ground
when suddenly
on some unspoken cue
flocks would rise in separate groups
and soar tight-knit loops
round car and lot
then settle down again.

Looking out my rain-drenched windshield
I saw a crow picking up a bit of stuff
was fully engaged in seagull's dance
of rising then dropping treasure
but it never could quite bring itself
to relinquishing the object
so up it flew
then down again
never really letting go.

A juvenile gull sidled up
preempting crow and nosing object
found it unworthy of a gull's indulgence.
"Silly birds," thought I
then remembering my own
thought better of my judgments.

In spite of the storm
or maybe because of it
a half-dozen dinghys came round the sea wall
eager for the tossing surf
sailors leapfrogging side to side
dodging sail, trying to ride
ocean swells like birds ride wind
fully charged from the squall
that appears to be nearing a flood.

December 16, 2001
Shilshole

Broken Patterns

The patterns of my days have been
further bent
first my son and now my friend
and she, so full of life
with loved ones many
removed from life against her will
mysterious intruder
drawing life's blood
with blade
across the rug,
across the floor
of the house that she had built.

The city was in turmoil
and nary a soul remained untouched
by this horrific event. Newscasters
twittered like coots seeing eagle
and police like canines searching for a scent
while the nervous flock regrouped
trying to find peace
in a fierce, fierce world.

Sinatra croons my favorite song,
"Have yourself a merry little Christmas,"
the strings and chorus following along
and I notice a line only dimly heard,
"if the fates allow,"

the stuff of life surrounding me
waitresses scurrying
and patrons smiling greetings
while I sit here writing so furiously
this page may ignite under pen.

December 20, 2001
Lake City

Jagged

Jagged, that's how I feel
with energies too big to fit
discomfort acute as I try to exist
casting about like a long-legged insect
legs tentatively reaching, seeking
but finding nothing solid.

Ready to explode, that's how I feel
with angry or sad, I'm not sure which
and at whom?
Now there's a mystery
I never will untangle.

The wind was high this afternoon
as I watched a crow
aloft and struggling,
storm buffeted to and fro
as it reached and strained
wings into wind
but made no headway
using every ounce of energy
just to hang, suspended.

Succumbing to the gale the crow
turned its head
and tumbled from the sky
grabbing for and anchoring on a pole
hunkering down to ride it out
grateful for a port in the storm.

Wisdom keepers help me heal
and find a way to ride this tempest
like a wind-whipped bird
struggling and losing
my circuit breakers must be broken
ante upping and upping I breathe it in
trying to absorb the flow
frantically
searching for a pole to sit.

December 20, 2001
65 Bus

Brief Encounter

Last night as I sat
there came
a sudden remembering
just there
it held me
in mind and body
wide awake,
alert
and deeply interested.

After it passed
I could find no trace
for the life of me
no recollection whatsoever
of what it was that felt so familiar
and so good— except the feeling
that for a moment
something
was very right with the world.

Today my sitting practice
sketchy as it is
has a bit more substance
the longing, beckoning
finally connecting
my eagerness renewed
another layer of significance
has been deeply woven in.

To the masters this will seem
a trifling incident
but believe me
with wild horses pulling
in a hundred directions
whatever takes me to the mat
is something very good.

December 21, 2001
Seattle

Line Disconnected

I would like to call my friend
and speak with her a while
but I can't
her line's been disconnected.

I would like to call her people
and speak with them a while
but I can't
their grieving is still a huddle
and my efforts have been denied.

Thrown back onto myself
energy building all the while
discomfort in my body
growing in magnitude
I struggle and wonder where
to put this bewildered energy?

Holiday invitations aplenty
interesting movies and food and music
and so many beautiful people
but I just don't fit

and end up seeking solitude.
Guess I'll watch the fire,
take a walk,
then come inside and sit.

December 21, 2001
Seattle

Empty Pages

I had a dream
that I was with my children
and so grateful to be with them
and someone
was it Colby?
was teaching me how
to wash the ink
off all my pages.

It felt good
and somehow deeply knowing
that to wash our pages
empty
is where we all
are going.

December 22, 2001
Seattle

It's not in Here

I stood in my living room
at a sudden loss and said,
"There's something that I'm looking for,"
and stood a moment in distress,
simply there, a state of emptiness
as I cast about for the thread
of what I was doing, ..."Oh yes!"
and reaching for the notebook
went to write a while, attempting to ease
the pressures in my head.

For many years I've struggled
trying to fill inner void
with every food scrap happening by
but it never could be filled.
Similarly afflicted
my friend put a reminder note
on every kitchen cabinet
reading, "It's not in here."

Having tried and failed
to fill the void with people
and continuing to build fantasies
around approaching strangers,
I've finally learned to help myself
by posting an imaginary note
on foreheads saying, "It's not in here, either."

Gardening is the closest I have come
to finding what I'm seeking
with beauty and wonder at every turn
and always gentle healing
but I hunger, still, for a connection deeper
such that I've had to admit
the answer to all my searching
is neither garden nor its creatures.

I fill my days with many deeds
earning a living, building community,
full of distracted energies
that draw me away from the deeper need
but once in a while I hit a spot, a vacuum
empty of activities and for a moment I recall,
"There's something that I'm looking for,"
and neither has it body nor flavor nor scent
nor does it crawl or slither or fly or think
nor is it made of ink
and yet, somehow,
it may be all of these.

December 22, 2001
Seattle

Daub

A daub of light is hanging
in a square of rainbow sky
spun from mist
draped near the setting sun
colors aloft and singing
accompanied by a full chorus of clouds.

The basses, dark and brooding below
flanked by staccato panels
of tenors and altos
while a single soprano soloist soars
a contrail of orange catching the sun
streaking across the sky.

The light on waves
rolls in toward marina
but the news barely penetrates this crowd,
hoards of hulls
layered in droves,
a density dissipating the obvious.

The rainbow drapes
like one passionate passage
in a vision by Phillip Glass
or perhaps it's the sutra of the heart
chanted in wavelengths
visible.

December 29, 2001
Winslow

Full Moon

The moon is full behind clouds of silk
that hide nothing, diminish nothing
as I stood on ferry deck
the shimmering sea went suddenly black
a tanker slipping across our bow
and I recalled Farley Mowat's vision:
two kinds of fog,
one encrusted with rivets.
My feet on deck and body on railing
felt the ferry's body straining

as suddenly, behind tanker one
came tanker number two,
a blackening slipping into view
fully six stories high would be my guess
and from my point of view
the only indication of its being
was a small square of light at water line
a portal to someone else's world
glimmering, shimmering on the sea
as if that square beam riding the waves

was a midnight sun from a world of angles.
Back home again keeping watch on deck
one year, almost, since he left
the rain is holding itself at bay
in honor of this lunar blessing
while a midnight Jupiter moves closer, too,

zenith in the firmament
and the world around is being bathed
soaking in celestial streams
and neither cats nor I can settle down.

December 29, 2001
Winslow Ferry

Anniversary – Day 365

I sought a quiet place by the sea
where I could honor your life
and your leaving
a year gone by this evening.
At first I tried to bring my friends
then realized they could not come here
with me
to this place of memories
but I am not alone
—the fire is alive and crackling
and the sea is nearly at my doorstep.
I arrived at sunset in time to greet friends
whose home it is I'm borrowing
and as they left I said to them,
"Thanks for all you've given me."

Shortly thereafter I was joined by the moon
coming up full and clear in the east
as I went to the market for dinner.
Then back to fetch firewood,
searching for the light,
easing down the stairs out into the dark
I went ahead thinking I'd feel my way
just like this whole year has been.
Tentacle feet tapping Braille underneath
I made slow headway till the corner
was reached
and there like a beacon illuminating the stack
was the moon and grinning
I laughed, "Thank you!"

Back inside noting hours slipping by
remembering how it went at just this time
every now and then I'd go outside
and monitor the moon crossing the sky
or down to the beach to note tide's exit west
slowly exposing bay flora and fauna
as well as a bevy of rivulets, fresh.

Rising over the house and hill
the moon was gradually swallowed up
by a colossal swirling system that
from where I stood on the edge of the sea
read like a gossamer flower
veil-like petal-puffs curled and distinct
shielding a star-studded sky
and for a moment or two it appeared
that the moon was the pivot
on which the heavens spun
like a glowing jewel peering out
from the middle
of a cosmic chrysanthemum.
This vision of stars and mist rose
with the moon
and gradually spun itself west
and watching from beach I looked up
and said,
"Thanks for all you've given me."

Back inside the hours sped past
as I listened to teaching tapes
those pearls of speech to help me gather
the wisdom of letting go

all the while my inner eye reviewed
a mind-bound video.
When time came to the hour you left
I tried to imagine how it went with you
and sat, this time breathing in your hurt
and mine of that time so full of anguish in
your absence
but my feelings are flowing
like moon's waxing and waning
and with each cycle I am reshaped
and with each dawn new, like you.

So, sitting with a single candle
and noticing how much has changed
I stayed awake as long as I could
there with the candle till it was ash before I
made for bed.
Looking outside I saw the moon hid
obscured by clouds grown very dense,
a blanketing, mending, dropping in meusk
and to the moon and rain, stars and pain
I turned saying,
"Thanks for all you've given me."

The fire was out as was the tide
and spent from watching wee hours crawling
I went and slept so peacefully
awaking at dawn thinking to review
last year in all words written
but instead am gazing at the bay,
gray from a cloudy, milky mist

transforming distant headlands
into freighters nosing darkly north
while cormorants and gulls are scouting
for breakfast.

Now tide is up and full to brim
and my dawn-lit fire is almost spent.
Am thinking I need to go back home
and start working a neglected garden
but for a few minutes more am going to sit
with a dawning rising from within
pausing a moment to say again,
"Thanks for all you've given me."

Mutiny Bay, Whidbey
December 30, 2001

Waking Vision

The cats awoke me
from a deep, deep sleep
and caring for them

opening door to deck
I went searching for the moon
barefooted

and finding, was bathed in light
a perfect fullness moon this night
a year from that you last walked in body.

As it moved cross the land
across an ocean of air and trees
across frozen toes and brow

and cloudy breath
a calming followed in its wake
washing sleep from eyes

and tears from chest and I felt
blessed by mystery teaching me
in ways I never could have guessed.

December 31, 2001
Seattle

January 2002

Colby's Bench

Light rings adorn the waves
puddles of energy caught by the sea
all blue-gray with a silver trim
from sunset over mountains.
Clear sky's a trace framed by ripples of mist
from a blanketing system moving in.
Snow-capped Olympics form a jagged crown
as ferryboat sentries are crossing the Sound
but in truth there is nothing marshal
about them,
all creatures mindful, absorbed in
their business.
The bay is full of log litter today
dark, horizontal glyphs riding low in the water
seeming hazardous but looking closer I see
birds strung in lines till they submerge
searching for bottom fodder.

I parked down the way a distance
wanting to find what I sought on foot
like the day I walked miles to Stonehenge
a gesture meant in reverence
for the mystery I would meet.
Seagull with a small black crab in its beak
eager juvi by its side
stopped feeding as I passed
looking anxiously at me
but finally resumed its task.

I'd been told the bench was finished
so I walked and searched
till the last stretch of headlands,
the last stretch of pines
and there, indeed, was a bench draped
in plastic.
I sat nearby keeping close company
and heard a strolling stranger say,
"I wonder what happened here?"
and almost called out,
"I will never know what happened
but can tell you the story,"
but didn't.

Sitting there feeling protective of the
curing process
I saw the cover obscured
but did not hide contents
of a new concrete pad and wooden bench
draped in white translucence.
Colby's bench, here at last
looking toward the mountains west
and up the passage north to the hillside
where your grandma's ashes rest
an exquisite panorama, infinite
next to the path where you bladed
with friends,
yes, this is a fitting tribute.

Unable to resist lifting sod chunks
holding plastic
I saw your plaque was not in place
that space filled instead by a template, blank.

The setting sun had all creatures restless
trying to glean essence from the fading light
as spinning system's separating strands
deep blue showing behind the gray
revealed the sun behind a cloudy shroud
illuminating twilight.
Lights are coming up around the bay
and the mountains are going black and I…
am packing up and heading home
taking a hint from all that lives,
growing into parting.

January 4, 2002
Alki

February 2002

Freeway

My home is a freeway,
cats coming
and going
all day and night long
and my heart is, too,
as feelings ebb and flow
sometimes getting
quite congested
all this traffic in my mind.

February 2, 2002
Seattle

Thin Ice

I understand if you cannot
approach me where I stand

on ice too thin to dance.
What I cannot fathom

is your pirouettes,
the vaulting, spinning

as you speed across ice
the same which holds me fast

approaching a point of breaking.
What riddle of illusion

keeps you in suspense
and how long,

I wonder, will it take
for the message to sink in?

February 8, 2002
Seattle

Not Worthy

I heard the call
and got the message
then felt my body fade
as I squirmed and searched horizon
for a means of some escape.

I cried,
"I am not worthy!"
but the message
now imbedded
was not one I could evade.

Struggling with myself
in doubt
searching inner being to find
just what was it
that I lacked

why, "not worthy,"
to be exact
when suddenly it dawned on me
this feeling had no link to worth
in truth I was afraid.

February 8, 2002
Seattle

Resistors

This living is a learning ground
and body, radio receiver
where every moment, day and night
transmissions come pouring in.

But this being seems resistant,
truly primitive equipment
distorting incoming signals
into pops and squeaks unreadable.

Dimly aware of energetic seedings
I patiently await the gleaning:
body chaff cast off at last,
essence, moonlike beaming.

February 8, 2002
Seattle

Candle

A candle dipped in melted wax
fruit born in blossom on a tree
things wrap themselves in layers
impossible to see.

All seeds slumbering deep within
encoding borne over seas of time
we wear in casual browns and greens
eyes sparkling fire, igniting being.

Salty essence circulating
memories of the sea
we often wear like pollen,
pollen riding on a bee.

Fire lighting wax and bee
is that which burns in me
illuminating all that is
a blazing reverie.

I am that fire burning
pyre glowing brighter, still
and every time when near the ocean
I feel more truly human.

Ocean coolness quenching
flames of craving and desire
sitting near the origin
I am one with Love's reply.

When seeded fuel has all played out
and having journeyed far enough
we'll reach a point of knowing
unbound by all we see.

February 20, 2002
Seattle

2:15 AM

What is this aching
waking me from dream?
Arising from within it seems
the gnawing nibbles at my being

tugging heart strings
till full attention is engaged.
Nothing will appease it,
nothing fills the gaping need

though I try and try
and try again
to stuff it or avoid it
or to go to sleep again.

When it comes my mind spins round
the reasons for its being
thinking this, or that
the source of so much pain

but if I simply sit with it
unfolding with the feelings,
perceive it deeper than I ever guessed
broader than my greatest failure

more vast than any sweet success
in fact it's not related
to any part of me,
it simply is the state of being

human after all,
this aching is the knowing
suffering lives in good and bad,
refuses to discriminate

laced through every happy-sad
enfolding all of life's unfolding
until we find the space
to let it go or hold it unattached

to meaning
or any measure of significance.
Suffering is—that's all
there is nothing more to grasp.

February 23, 2002
Seattle

Perhaps

Perhaps it's not an easy thing
standing outside looking in
to fathom how it feels
to have lost a love to suicide,
perhaps the gnawing grieving
does not clamor at your being
nor can you look
and see the battle raging as raw feelings

vie for my attention
asserting reasons for my failing.
Perhaps the sense of utter loss
has never visited your doorstep
nor the lingering doubts
suggesting the one stone left unturned,
the one road never taken,
was the one that could have saved him.

Perhaps the act of sitting
with the pain of never knowing,
loss beyond all measure
bending body under weight
of tear-stained bed sheets
and mornings yawning aching
perhaps the mystery of this living
has not yet opened you.

Perhaps events have yet to peel your heart
or stretch it till it bursts
and you've not yet found yourself
discarded on a lonely shore
with other storm-tossed broken fragments

perhaps the juice that flows
across your synapse
is not yet charged with sadness.
Perhaps the gift of your humanity
has not yet dawned on you.

February 23, 2002
Seattle

Spinning Ink

This spinning of ink across a page
from the wool of deepest yearning
this forming of words
from fragments curling
streaming conceptual bridge

this casting of line
into pools of connecting
is driven,
ever driven it seems
by a breath that is being breathed.

February 23, 2002
Seattle

Silky

Not quite suited to this world
this human happening
wild thing residing in your heart
making its way all awkwardness
of silky bound in human body
you would prefer to be adrift
on frigid ocean liquid swift
sleekness playing with the waves
or to drape yourself languidly across
a warming rock to rest

this humanness craving
softness and companionship
does not suit you,
unaccustomed to comfort
it is not a quality you crave
but to be taken by the longing
as if seized by eagle soaring,
searching,
steady gaze locked on subject
in tune with seasons turning
and all ordinary things deeper,
I suspect it is this
would feed your hunger.

February 28, 2002
Seattle

March 2002

Awakening

Delicate lace of bare limbs in streetlight
skeletal structure
with new growth emerging
bursting forth in cascading flowers
incandescent glowing colors
against the dark and warming gray of bark.

Look about!
see hillsides turning
ribbons of subtle color
willows wrapped in burning umber
and swaths of ruddy, red alder
the first to come in spring

limbs rousing from their slumber
and like sun's dawning
raw with color
trees alive
as you and me,
reaching toward awakening.

March 25, 2002
Seattle

April 2002

April

The seasons are turning
round again
April is here
bringing snow in the mountains
and this morning my breath
blew away in clouds
like mist rising off the sea.

April 8, 2002
Seattle

Clouds

Water-soaked cotton fluffs
inching snail-like across the sky
humped up high and round
with dark, flattened feet
across an invisible density
clouds form a patchwork quilt, light
and dark over desert dry
across slopes ribbed
like a sleeping giant's body
articulated muscular strength
worked by rain and wind
and clad in polka-dot stretch fabric
of artemisia, sage and lichen.

Every muscle crease is darkened with green
where dew rolls like sweat off hillsides
into the rolling, tumbling Columbia
going to join a salty sea.
Beneath the sensuous rolling hills
exposed by eons of rivers running
are bones of volcanoes layered up
columnar rocky fragments
once liquid and flowing building of hills
in successive molten, blanketing waves
covering all in sheets of rock.

Sitting here watching the clouds snail by
watching a river bent to our will
looking at landforms, weather tilled

I see life as if in an hourglass jar
the flowing erosion of hour to hour
turning mountains to dust and all life to ash
as snail clouds and I go sailing by
shaped by the space in which we stand
molded to fit the air we breathe
being breathed by an endless wind.

April 14, 2002
Columbia River

Phone Call

I get letters addressed to you
and grandma, too,
not a terrible inconvenience
these reminders riding envelopes
filling my world with feelings.

And do you know I still get calls?
Today a voice asked for you and I,
with a twinge of incredulity asked,
"Who is this?..."
a year and four months since you left.

And today down the drive
I saw something new,
little dwarf maple, lacey limbs weeping
was covered in newly emerging leaves
dripping life as they unsheathe,

last year, did I miss this?
I don't remember noticing sweetness, newness
busily beginning again, driven by life's urgency
after the stillness of winter.

And look! Blue sky is framing green of trees
and cherry blossoms, as hummer bees
cruise and bumble about my yard.
Had to gingerly pick one up

allowing legs to grasp my glove
so full of spring's exuberance it bumped

into my car so I took it to a rhodi blossom
where legs, searching for solid bottom,
dreamily attached.

I do not remember last year's spring.
How could I have missed it?
Absorbed in grief it simply passed
as I bumbled about my business.

April 18, 2002
Seattle

Yellow Bowl

I bought it years ago
almost twenty-four in fact
across the street from the hospital
at an old-fashioned dime store
a yellow plastic bowl.
Unlike most plastic of that time
this was thick and smooth and beautiful
gleaming in the light.

Bowl firm and solid in its weight
and generous of proportions, perfect
for holding fruit nearby
as I sat for over a fortnight.
They said they couldn't be sure,
indeed, not until you journeyed back
was a diagnosis even possible.

This round there was no chance
no getting better
no end of pain
no cycling there and back again
your end brought home in brutal impact
—life spilling over no longer held fast
your body an empty container.

I took your meds and filled the bowl
the colors forming a veritable rainbow
and such a fullness! A pharmacist's dream
of health and well-being
that never found a match

then went and flushed them down
feeling close to following after.
Today this kitchen where I stand
has stood sixteen months in your absence
and yellow bowl is filled again
with apples, oranges and bananas
as I sit with where I am
staying steady with the pain
watching the cycles spin and spin
basking in the afternoon heat
eating a piece of fruit.

April 20, 2002
Seattle

Old

She asked when it was
I began to feel "old"
a rhetorical question about life's pain
from one young enough to long for none
and perplexed by the ever growing pain
mounting her youthful body.
I told her, "Old came when I lost my son
and lost my will to live,"
but there was more I could not tell,
more I could not give
for I've learned "old"
does not always come with age—
think of those grinning octogenarians
who are still in love with living.
Indeed, only youth can be very "old"
so old there is a giving up
imagining there is something else,
some other way to feel,
some other place to be,
where pain and hardship don't exist.

Aging comes to all who live
but "old" is a wallowing, muddy mind-set
where we allow ourselves to languish.
Seeing this now I know my task
life's journey beckoning as I stand
stuck fast
uncertain, frightened and burdened
but a seed has been implanted

from the mind-stream of luminous wisdom
just like seeded lotus
in swamp's deepest muck
from that depth the growing starts
emerging at the surface tranquil
an exquisite, radiant flower at last.
The storyline brings the gnawing grieving
but without that thread
it's just my feelings
uncomfortable, difficult to be sure
but something I can deal with.
There is a dawning coming to me
as I pause to grasp deep wisdom
letting go while standing fast
a paradox like all the rest
but this one's reworking my love of life
helping me rejoin the living.
Years may go by as I learn to cope
for nothing on this journey is easy or quick
but now I am quite certain
this way will be my path.

April 20, 2002
Seattle

Bird Song

The sound that pulled was high and thin
a mysterious loon-like longing
in first light's rays of dawning.

For several days I've heard the call
winging rings around my world
it made me dizzy trying to follow.

For several days I've tried to spy
this phantom greeting,
flying by

gracing all with pre-dawn reed song
like moonbeams
shimmering on water.

Today I held my hands up high
to block the beacon lighting lot
and saw a gleaming,

silver flash
as dawn's streams caught it
streaking past

singing circles round the morn
enlightened song
that touched my being.

April 28, 2002
Lake City Bus Stop

May 2002

Emerald Dawn

The morn was dark
the dawn delayed
by a heavy, spongy,
sodden blanket.

The road was wet
in such a way
the street light beamed
and spilled across

as if we'd lost
a can of paint
glowing brilliance
on shimmering black

and gazing down
the road I saw
a bed of emeralds
set in asphalt.

May 2, 2002
Seattle

Awake!

Take the sleep from your eyes
the cotton from your ears
arise! and join the morning.

Take a walk on a beach
where seas of rippled sand
stand firm as mountain ridges

and pulverized plants
float in tannish clouds
through rivers running between.

Slip toes into water and feet,
feel sand fish scurry, darting fleet
avoiding that embrace.

May 18, 2002
White Rock, BC

Gem Stone

Coming round the corner
and up the familiar
narrow path

crushed gravel's
chiseled angles crunching
under steel-toed boots

scuffling through
the dusty gray of mid-day
on our way to lunch

full of purpose—empty stomachs
my eyes read incongruity
which stopped me in my tracks.

Shimmering jewel-like
in that ordinary space
was a curiosity, smoothly black,

polished lustrous and nested
in such a way
it seemed to have been placed.

Kneeling to examine
wonder waiting for my glance
I found a pebble

darkly granite
and much like all the rest
except the rounded fullness

was soaking, streaming wet,
glowing with a brilliance
awaking me from slumber.

May 23, 2002
Seattle

Rainbow Puddle

A rainbow puddle is crawling
across my kitchen floor
so odd in shape it caught me
rushing out the door

mid-step, out of breath
letters and bills and laundry
I whirled, almost gone
till the light grabbed hold of me.

It formed an irregular pastel circle
banded violet, purple, blue, pale green
then a center lit but neutral
followed by yellow, orange, a hint of red.

I reached down to catch it in my hand
to find the source of so much strangeness
allowing colors to run into my palm
I lifted it and walked in such a way

the shimmering, banding draped across
my arm
and there it merged with me,
blue of veins and purple, too,
subtle colors blending in

could hardly tell where rainbow ended and
I began.
Made my way across the room
tracing light streams back to skylight,
wiggling fingers, checking angles

till light and shadows intertwined
and came to sit right in the middle
as colors pooled across the floor
then jumped upon our dining table

where resting palm and fingers bathed
in a many colored stream
so soft in hue I gazed and saw
the radiant luminescence of my paw.

May 23, 2002
Seattle

Dawning

Daylight at the bus stop
and the just past full

moon is setting over the body shop.
Pink accents color stationary clouds

high above gray cover
moving swiftly north.

I've found a place of song to share
a place to join with friends

and a dawning from within that knows
the real work now begins.

May 28, 2002
Lake City Bus Stop

One Simple Thing

How am I doing?
I'd be glad to say

if only I knew,
if only I could somehow connect.

Time passing with speed
there is one simple thing I need

but it seems to be eluding me
it simply is not solid.

May 31, 2002
Seattle

Another Spin

The cycle has turned another spin
I'm here again, exhausted,
unhinged,
wandering a life
that reads like a dreamy newsreel
as I watch, casually,
and muse…

how do I go to work
and come back home again
how did I navigate that turn
how make the car stop in time
how notice when my turn in line
how be with those I cannot feel
how manage to make another meal?

May 31, 2002
Seattle

June 2002

Symphony

I awoke to the sounds
of the sweetest symphony
rain, pattering on my roof
like little frogs
lily pad leaping

metronome drone
steady drip, drip, drop,
leaky gutter marking time

while birds sang
counterpoint melody
robins in tune with
starlings' trill
as a crow landing
in the driveway below
let out a percussive
squawk.

June 2, 2002
Seattle

July 2002

OK?

A tentative dream-like haze
accompanies me these days.

I rest in a state of fuzzy distraction
where the making of plans seems

pure abstraction
and my expression betrays a blankness,

dazed
by a world that is coming unraveled.

Friends say, "Are you OK?"
and their question puzzles me.

July 4, 2002
Seattle

Tears

Standing to honor his son just wed,
raising a cup of joy in toast
I heard this gentle friend proclaim
that he was just "the hardware man,"

all gratitude was due his wife and love
the one who taught them softness.
Reaching for his younger son
who'd asked him, "Why?"

the tears he saw
I heard him trying to explain
the tears that somehow always fall
at every rite of passage

when even during times of bliss
when joy seems near to crushing us
our cheeks are traced in trails of salt
our eyes brimful with sadness

so he spoke of birth and hope
and hearts so full of joyful glad
they lift and bubble up
and brimming, spill right over top.

Sitting there it came to me,
"Don't forget the tears of grief
for lives we've lived and all lives lost,"
and thought, perhaps, to raise a toast

to pain and death, despair and loss
by which all brimful hearts are broke
and flood our brimful lives with tears,
love borne through human hardship.

Fearing I might foul the feast
I finally stood and left the place
where so much joy had gathered
as tears began to rise in me

a gnawing, soreness welling up
for a love, now dead
and dreams that followed
of what our lives would be.

Later, as I sat to think,
"What are these tears, and what's the link?"
I saw so clearly through the dark
our hopeful, fearful bargaining

imagining we could somehow cleave
cloud from sky and sun from rain,
remove ourselves from suffering
but in these fields of paradox

both joy and pain are born of love
and inside each there is the other
there is no way to separate
what love has cleaved together.

In this living, breathing dream
arising from our greatest sum
a knowing dawns from deep within
that joy and pain are simply one.

Stranger still we come to know
that only broken cuts right through
confusion claiming either/or
all visions of duality.

When we finally let them be
the tearful seeds we sow in love
will one day blossom, free at last,
made whole through deep compassion.

July 5, 2002
Oakland, California

Stretching

My mind
stretching

across an ocean
of time

eons
of space

has finally found you
here in my heart.

July 13, 2002
Seattle

It's Time

It's time to let you go, I know,
the dream I had it told me.
Inside the box
fingers sifting through gray
I grasped your face,
a death mask of bone
and wafer thin
like finding chards of porcelain
looking as if you simply slept
eyes closed so peacefully.
What were you doing in that place?

It's time to let you go, I know,
I finally found the strength
to open box
and grasp the bag
clear plastic holding your remains
held firmly to my breast
so heavy as I sat
rocking on my zafu.

It's time to let you go, I know,
The men have already left.
I heard them say, "Those ashes
are not truly he—they hold
no meaning at all,"
remarks that stunned and flattened me
searching for compassion.

It's time to let you go, I know,
a peaceful letting go at last
ashes scattered on the sea
as compassion finds a home in me
there is no other option.
No matter where I turn in search
the mirror stares right back.

July 28, 2002
Seattle

Crow Morning

Sometimes I miss it
in the dark.
A single crow just flew past
a radiant half-moon
a little to my right
suspended in a wire grid
outside of which
are legions of them
dressed in black and full of haste
winging their way across the grid
off to their morning meeting.

Dawn approaching in the east
seems sun is coming to meeting, too.
"Where do they go?" I wonder,
seeing them at dawn
heading south and away
thousands and thousands in loosely knit ranks
blazing trails across dark cloud banks
all dressed in Friday casuals.

July 31, 2002
Lake City Bus Stop

August 2002

Dizziness

The dizziness has returned.
I stoop to focus

and when I lift my gaze
the world is spinning round.

Luckily
the bushes caught me.

August 3, 2002
Seattle

Can I Possibly?

Can I possibly
ever
get used to this?
Might as well try walking
on that Mylar seeming sheet
waving dizzily toward me
stretched tight and slightly curved
any walking there
would be up
and up, wave top
to wave top.

The sun has gone but the sea is lit
by summer evening's twilight
and radiant Venus is rising nearby
as the day is tipping into dark.
The way is somewhere near, I'm sure,
looking will surely find it.

The walkway turned gracefully
round and round,
baluster, stair stepping solidly down
and down they go
till they submerge
and down and down my eyes still peer
as if at some lost, ancient artifact,
Atlantis rising from the deep
as stairs and rail come climbing back.

Nary a soul walks here tonight
perhaps avoiding the lap,
lap, lapping erosion
of all we take for real.

August 29, 2002
Alki

September 2002

Something About

There is something about
launching things into existence,

something that lives
to witness the effect.

The day is gray,
cloudy and cold

and still we line up,
parents and toddlers

reaching out,
building bridges

at earth's joining with water,
parents modeling

tossing pebbles into the waves
their babies following exactly.

Two days ago, I sat on Colb's spot
and watched as a neighbor

calmly lined up his shot
then drove several

golf balls
into the bay.

September 1, 2002
Alki

Herringbone

Herringbone beach print,
notes jotted down and kept,
minutes taken as tide receded
from early morning meeting.
The day is just dawning
as wings aflutter, gaping maw
young crow bends low
in submission to its hunger.
Sea birds edging lower
work the line between
as water slips down
the polished, pebbled reach
out to the drowned echo
of a sandy beach.
Pigeons are digging up top
beaks flying busily this way and that
while gull with a clam the size of my fist
is standing on sidewalk,
calmly drops it as I laugh
but that small gap renders
a delectable feast.
A wave heaves up suddenly
over the beach
making clear what was hidden before
like a point, briefly made,
in the conversation they keep.
Then it's gone, wave
along with the rivulets draining,
dragging hourglass sand

through the canyons created
showing satellite views
of miniature Rio Grandes
one wave and its gone,
every precipice, every winding,
every caprice of artery tracing now
flowing past to the future,
deep lines marking shoreline
like the lines on our faces
erased in a moment with nary a trace
and now it's starting to build again
as sea birds afloat search tender morsels.

Septmeber 1, 2002
Alki

Calendula Harvest

Tan bracts curled round
like mandibles

or hairy spider legs
protective

almost menacing
as center sat

the dark brown seedlets
curled up tight

with finely toothed scrimshaw
scrawled across their backs.

Organic creature
living being

round and round
the petals leaving

new cycle held
within the last.

September 5, 2002
Seattle

Italian Plum

Love's blush on plum
fuzzy, glowing bloom

like an eager heart
leaping from its breast

in greeting
I went to wash it off,

acknowledgment,
and calmly stood there eating.

Every day a dawning comes
one with all the rest,

ageless essence ever present
in everything we see and do

every leaf aflutter
every drop of mist

every heart that's broken
and in breaking is renewed

I feel that fuzzy bloom afresh
heart song in my breast.

Septmeber 13, 2002
Seattle

Here

Though many pearls
are cast our way
we only harvest
those we heed

seeds of lives we've lived before
remnants woven by thought and deed
into the fabric of our days
a winding, spooling, reeling dream

and me, no different
fundamentally
from you or she
who began this journey

coming to see
that in this
here
is everything we need.

September 15, 2002
Seattle

Letting Go

At first I could not open it
those ashes in a box
took a year and a half
to find my way
to prying up the hatch
screwdriver free
rendering first glance.

I held them tight
these fragments wrapped
up to my breast
while rock-a-bye baby
sitting on the floor
I held them for a spell
then gently put them back.

Once opened the box
remained ajar
it would not close again
so happenstance has joined them
with my sitting practice
ever opening to gray in clear plastic
as months go flying by.

They stay the same but somehow
I have changed
for fear no longer holds me fast
seeing them now

I think of winter nights
hearthside sitting cozily
fire glowing, burning bright
indeed, those ashes are not he

and I am content with this
only occasionally
wondering
how long it will be
till ashes find their way
to the sea.

September 15, 2002
Seattle

DIZZY

Awoke this morning dizzy,
dizzy,
one foot, two feet
planted firmly
trying to cross the floor
I felt in imminent danger
of crashing into walls.
Reeling head spin hoped
sitting would surely settle me
and it did
somewhat
but when I arose
the world was spinning,
spinning,
dancing me on toes
so much I dared not ride my bike
but drove
and bus stop waiting
saw the stars,
Orion in his usual pose,
power lines bisecting
as the world was turning,
turning,
spinning me
and setting moon in full regalia
gracing all with luminosity
it dawned on me,
"What is this place I call my home?

How do I rise and greet each morn?"
spinning, spinning daily threads
following glowing tracings
that mimic something solid.

September 20, 2002
Seattle

Painting

For its warmth I choose the darkened red
a radical departure from my usual crisp white
then noticed it splashed across
late summer sunsets
and fall's passion
painting Liquidambar limbs.

The red we share no matter our color
the red of love and that of anger
and too, my teacher's robes
simple and sacred
indeed, the shade of blood.

Radiant pigment
reminder of impermanence
taken to heart as I lean against an absence,
the opposing white wall,
carefully cutting in
the edge.

September 22, 2002
Seattle

Solace

The log was shaped
like an arm curved round my shoulders
or a sleeping,
spooning torso
but these comforts
do not draw

it is the sea that beckons me
to breathe,
to join the whistling wind
and wander with wave's booming echo
rolling slowly down the beach,
to revel in the rankness of rotting kelp,
steep in sweet scent of salt.

Like a wild creature's
deepest instinct,
a wayward, wounded mammal
this is the only way to help
when feeling lost and frantic.
Whenever I cannot find my way
my feet gather me up
and bring me here,
this place, my only solace.

September 27, 2002
Alki

Sea Frock

Leaning against
the storm tossed trunk
I squirm a little
nest in sand,
a shorebird
reading tidal signs,
and nestle in amidst the strands
of seaweed pearls
forgotten

notice sea frock
nosing up
the gently curving, sandy beach
spread thin like silky satin
clinging
to a heaving breast-line,
come to seek
the treasures lost
when frock
fell from yesterday's body.

September 27, 2002
Alki

Waves

Have you ever noticed
waves always greet shore
at an angle?
No matter the twists
and turns of beach
at any place along the line
the meeting will be oblique
slipping in between the troughs
the forces never squared at ninety.

No matter where you are,
what state you're in
somewhere deep
our bodies know
while thinking mind
lingers round the bend,
yet to feel the impact.

It's a kindness when in trauma
this distance that we keep
imagining ourselves separate—
while wave upon wave
washes our shores
and minds are left to grieve
our bodies slowly work it through,
the knowing held within.

September 27, 2002
Alki

Promenade

She walked like a knife blade
piercingly thin
with a chin that read like an anvil
but I know we're the same,
my cushioned softness
armor
and just like her edges, an attempt
to fend off all onslaughts.

I see now no difference, offense,
defense
both nurtured,
intertwined
and breed of ignorance.

September 27, 2002
Alki

Shadow Player

Shadow player in a puppet world
city dweller seeking the sea
I come here occasionally.
No one sees me,
a passing stranger,
casually surveying the beach
while sitting crone-like on a bench
hunched over my notebook's
curled-finger scrawl.

Beach fires reflecting on gathering faces
serious walkers striding briskly by
bladers' and bikers' bodies toiling
meandering strollers and I—not unfriendly
this distance, just anonymous
under street lights
as planes overhead roar
on their way to a runway.

Shadow players, all
as we craft our dramas
playing them out
over pages with lines
moving in rhythm, moving in rhyme
drifting through space
like tide drawn beach bottles
breathing the ebbing
and flowing of time.

September 27, 2002
Alki

Midwife

Something is coming.
The air around me is pregnant
and the sea is crashing expectantly
swollen curves carrying
each wave to shore
umbilical cord cloud
curling off at horizon.

Like a midwife
I'm waiting
on something
I know not what
hoping it will arrive shortly
like the moon
through soft folds of cloud
a natural birth,
straightforward.

I sit
an eager readiness
as beach pebbles hum
a restless tune.

September 27, 2002
Alki

November 2002

Claws

Claws on street in swirling circles
halting jerky skittering
scurrying, leaping,
cartwheeling by

stuttering motion catches eye
alerting and alarming me
as if driving a road
chock full of crabs and frogs.

But it's only oak and maple leaves
like curled and painted parchment
blown dry after the morning rain
by swiftly passing cars.

The sky is dark and thickly looms
a heaviness shifting and slipping such
that last light seems at first to leer
then gently smile at me.

But it's only storm clouds moving past
clearing paths for moonbeams
as I note the signs and make a story
that somehow reads to me.

November 8, 2002
Lake City

Squirrelly Again

What is it that I'm feeling?
Jagged and squirrelly and reeling
I seem to have once again
lost my way.

The rains have finally come back through
and perhaps memory's body
is recalling
what it was to have newly lost you.

The distance to my nearest neighbor
might be an eternity,
rain pelting loudly on my roof
fir needles stopping up all the drains.

There is no fix to this
but sitting very quietly
I find some relief
some semblance of serenity

letting go the story
letting go the grief
letting go the anger
that would destroy me.

Sitting, sitting
and taking it in—rain and sirens
and distant friends.
Letting it be

just as it is
with some measured dregs of sanity
amidst a whirling ship at sea
going down all around me.

November 16, 2002
Seattle

Part Knows

Part knows
his leaving served me,
stands simply in acknowledgment
of the gift
come through the door
that cataclysmic opening
to compassion deeper
than I could have ever known.

And then comes the crushing
when stilled by the loss of a son
waves of grief roll over me
tossing, tumbling, rendering
a flotsam jumble of flesh and bones
soaking in a salty sea
of loss born of remembering.

So back and forth I lurch along
an awkward, struggling human being
making my way through laughter and tears
and the sharing we do as we gather years
no up, no down,
no here and gone
weaving all into a fabric, living
that looks like you and me.

You ask me how I do it,
how find the joy within the pain

and I say to you from where I sit
there is no loss
there is no gain,
just the sharing of our humanity.

November 25, 2002
Seattle

December 2002

Gray Day

This bench,
it cradles me
and softly waving sea in front
colors subtle
fills my heart
along with today's scent of salt
seeming almost intangible.

Dark sail cuts a triangular wedge
into the mountains distant
and darkened ships are buoying up
cargo white and cargo black
snailing tracks across the bay
with ferries swiftly parting.

The wind at my back
gently ruffles my hair
in a scene set in shades of gray
while the sea shines
with a brilliance, lit
in luminous greens
and blues arrayed
rising up from the sandy bottom.

December 1, 2002
Alki

Where Are You With It?

She asked, "Where are you with it?"
and I tried to answer honestly
with words that might
explain
but couldn't
for I felt in her query
a barricade
halting attempt
to shield her from the pain
and somehow keep it distant.

Not in words but there,
palpably, in her fear
bracing against the intensity of loss
so many shy away from
that is now my hearth and home
for I have come to know
he is always near
as sadness ebbs and flows
and I find my way
through life's broad tidal washes
sitting, walking,
on the path
to deepening compassion.

December 3, 2002
Seattle

Credentials?

Indeed, one might ask
what right have I
to assert myself
what layering on
of education

and experience
could possibly
give me the temerity
to post these words upon a page
and ask that others share them?

And I could make a list,
the ivy league schools, those degrees
of singularity, that verity
many take as proof of worth
but I'll tell you now how it seems to me.

For all the living years gone by
the piling up of things and deeds
layering on incessantly
promises of safety
and security

it was not until the day
there came to me a stripping away,
a peeling, coring,
laying bare and opened
that true worth dawned on me.

December 21, 2002
Seattle

February 2003

If Only

Even now, two years gone by
I sit and ponder how
and why
and conjure up, "If only."

If only I had stopped mid-track
and ventured further in our search
if only I had taken him
to the ends of the earth
and back

if only I had lost the cats
sold it all
every shingle and stick
and steered my little family
to a place far away
from trouble.

If only…

And then I come to where
I see
the dream amidst reality,
grabbing the reins
of lives I've loved
to steer them
somehow
safely home.

Februray 6, 2003
Seattle

More Than This

More than this,
(or is it less?)
I daub eyes with bed sheet
and turn
waiting for it to pass,
the wave that just swept through.

One could read it as sadness
I often do
maybe with a twinge of anger
or maybe simply pain

but it's more than this,
no matter how I look
it's more
more than all the feelings
I could ever find a name for
larger, fuller
more real.

Trying to fit this into logic
the numbers don't add up
this place where words
and feelings shed away
as well as what I pine for.

February 26, 2003
Seattle

Jammies

You have become part of us
like yesterday's laundry
worn thin, comfortable
ever-present.
You hang about me in the jammies
I've taken to wear
soft, brown-plaid flannel
the elastic in the leg
binds a little
at my ankle.

And your brother, too,
is wearing you.
I saw your thread-bare
boxers in the laundry
when he came home from school.
Not a word was spoken,
there was no need to.

February 26, 2003
Seattle

Appendix 1: Notes from 2001

In the beginning my body could barely stand the flow, energy full blown in solar plexus and belly. Then it moved to my heart and head, spinning, churning, opening. Through the top of my head I felt a tremendous current, up, down, I'm not at all sure of the direction. I was a paradox – a full vacancy; completely emptied and yet filled beyond brim with surging energy forcing a quieting, softening, stillness upon me. Old wounds healed instantly, all trespasses forgiven. In a way never before possible I could listen beyond all former impressions, taking others in undirected and unedited and then, completely drained, I would hastily retreat to the quiet of solitude.

For me, time seemed to have stopped and my connection to earth was threadbare and tenuous. The world was spinning way too fast and every fiber of my former existence was stretched beyond its limits. Catapulted to a place where I could barely move, I found my mind was completely blank and body suddenly old and feeble. Every other moment I was forced to gather my derelict wits and consider what were my intentions in this place? Why I was standing by the bathroom sink—was I there to brush my teeth? Of course, that was it! A short while later this process would repeat as I'd find myself standing in the middle of the kitchen. Why am I here? Oh, yes… a cup of tea…

I'd lost all continuity and with each laborious step nothing could be taken for granted, routine and habits blown away in an instant, that instant Death walked up our doorstep in the form of public servants heavy laden with their tragic news of Colby. Driving I avoided but if circumstances forced it I drove very slowly, gripping the wheel, flummoxed at every intersection, severely challenged by all surrounding and hi-speed inputs. A trip to the grocery was clearly out of the question as the intensity of simple interactions and advertising graphics was enough to blow all my circuits. Besides, I could not begin to think of cooking a meal, in food I'd lost all interest.

Now and then I came upon small flowers oddly in my path, on the stair, in the empty cassette case of a tape that I was playing – a tape I'd used repeatedly never noticing any flora and suddenly it held a single, fresh forsythia flower. Once after an upsetting telephone conversation I rose up quite distracted and returning several minutes later found a small purple straw flower in the middle of the cushion. Flowers like those I'd put on the place he'd ended life, and every time it happened I felt a presence that brought me back to life from the depths of my
deep sadness.

Traumatic loss is brutal in its effect but grief can come in many guises whenever our lives meet change, demanding of us a new response to living. And all grieving has a biological process of its own, like old age or adolescence, and if you find yourself in its presence, chances are there will be some who cannot join you.

Truly wishing to be of help friends and loved ones say, "Call me anytime," and then they're gone. And do I call? Maybe one or two who have always understood me and they always ask, "How you doin'?" but trying to explain my state is crazy-making for words do not exist to help them see if life has not yet led them on the journey. Like a long distance runner in the middle of a marathon or a molting insect casting an outgrown existence or a solo sailor struggling to survive a storm, I had no energy to spare in bringing them on board.

"Don't tie yourself in knots like this!" he said and I believe his appeal was genuine. I replied, "I'm not tying knots, I'm unraveling them." And thought to myself, "He refuses to feel. Indeed, he comes from a long line of people who have buried their feelings before they were dead." He was probably thinking that I wear my heart on my sleeve unnecessarily. I could have gotten all bent out of shape by this, taking his comments as an attack at worst and at best, a cold-hearted sentiment. But Death opened a window in me that was so broad, the breeze just blew through and I noticed how old resentments, even those I'd once nourished, vanished.

People for whom I had once held resentment came by and I would greet them quietly where I sat, firmly planted. I remember feeling appreciative of their presence, their thoughtfulness in coming. My heart was free, perhaps holding so much pain there was no room left. But that wasn't it for the pain had not yet started, and I felt truly free of old entrapments. All that energy spent on misunderstandings! Suddenly I could be with old friends as if at a new beginning, all the while acutely aware of feeling a deep fondness for them and every process, good and bad, that we had ever shared.

Before Death came the understanding that we choose to hold a grudge or not was so highly theoretical I never gave it a second glance, preferring instead to cling to hurts and times of sadness like a pouting child with a broken play toy clings to misery. Imagine how amazed I was to find myself without fear or anger, without space or time tangents, conscious only of fiercely spinning energy, hot-wiring me to a new beginning empty of everything I'd ever used to define my reality. The extraordinary openness that I was for a while eventually passed and was replaced by more familiar habits, but a reference point was now implanted like a compass rose anchored to the center of my being, and with it came a knowing that we choose which way we go, toward anger or forgiveness.

Thirteen months have passed since my son's death, and I feel a slow healing brewing. I am better. I go to the grocery without elaborate planning and purchase what I want to eat as if I had some interest in it. This is new. Before I had no interest in things, no ability to conceive a thought or follow it through, feeling like a shell with edges indistinct, housing only a deep longing that never could be filled and a pain in my heart that was crushing me. Now, from the perspective of some distance as I try to understand my own and others' reactions to this crisis, I have arrived at a point where I see there is no way to wrongly grieve. We give life and death whatever we can and it does not hurt me that others are different. There is no need to change to suit another's preference. Each does the best she or he can and whatever understanding grows out of our intentional or inadvertent sharing is a gift. The rest I must do on my own.

I know now very few can help when tragedy walks up your doorstep, and I need to be gentle with myself and gentle with everyone else in this place of no real roadmaps. All gratuitous judgments from "How can they be so unfeeling?" to "How can she be so effusive?" need to go, replaced by a little compassion. Everyone wants us to mirror them, to be just like, or mimic some supposed measure of progress but I cannot be other than what I am. Give all the advice in the world, it will not help. If you want to help, what I truly need is for you to sit with me and listen – nothing to fix, nowhere else to be – just here with all our feelings.

Healing comes when we share from the heart, spreading all of our cards on the table. Some cannot go there with you, who find sitting with another's pain frightening as if they might catch it or worse yet, feel their own which they've spent a lifetime avoiding. I cannot judge them harshly. We do the best we can, all of us, including those ending life prematurely. The point is to be there for each other while letting go of judgments. Since Colby's death I've learned life is more complex than I could have ever dreamed, with layers that are not immediately obvious, rendering superficial judgments not just unhelpful, but downright ludicrous. With this awareness in mind I am trying with all my heart to sweep my path clear of clutter, the chatter pro and con, gratefully accepting what support comes to me and giving back what I can.

There were times when I lamented about the kind of people who change aisles in the grocery when they see you coming. In fact, just last summer at lunch with a friend I spoke to her of my frustration with those who run from sadness saying, “People are afraid of death.”

And she told me, “They don’t want to hurt you.”

I asked, “How could it hurt, speaking of death?”

She said, “By making you remember.”

So I replied, “How could remembering hurt?”

She answered, “They want you to forget the pain.”

I asked, “Why?”

“Because it hurts!” she cried but I could not understand, knowing the pain and memories never leave, and speaking of it, and even the tears were a comfort from where I sat. So she tried again to help me by explaining

it from a different tack saying, "It
hurts them to see you in pain like it hurt you to see
Colby suffering."

At last a light dawned and I saw anew
the message that he sent,

There is beauty even in fear and pain
but visible only to those deeply submerged in it.

I finally saw and understood my failure toward him, to not be able to stand his pain and instead to fiddle and fuss around it; so difficult for me to witness his trauma standing outside, looking in. I had to be rubbing his back or reading aloud a book, trying with all my might to cure him. Perhaps it's fair to forgive myself, knowing how impossible it would be for any mother to share her child's pain in a manner unattached, but from my present vantage I see it very differently. I'm not looking for cures like those promised by distractions or avoidance; this pain is too deep inside me. Clearly, for what ails me now there is no simple fix.

Humans recoil from pain, even more theirs than yours. We fear it, and cannot be near it, and when we see a loved one in pain, we need to fix it fast. But some pain cannot be fixed and must be lived as it re-works our way of being. In cases like this instead of avoidance a steady listening is needed. There are few who are equipped to handle this, few who can bear another's pain with compassion and loving kindness. They are somehow

evolved beyond the rest, perhaps by virtue of pain
they've processed; but whatever is true about their gifts,
I wish for you who are suffering that you may find at
least one like them among your caregivers and friends.

And when people wonder aloud if you are "over it yet"
I've learned to gently ask if they are "over" the births
of their children and grandchildren or "over" their
first kiss? All life's events leave their mark, happy
or sad, no difference. Look around you! Each of us
carries those marks in countenance, mind and body.
With every new event or change there is potential
for growth toward greater compassion and wisdom
if we can let them in. The death of a loved one, or
illness, or birth, weaves into our life's fabric in lasting
strands that forever color the tapestry that is us.

If you are suffering loss, for whatever reason, seek
out others who can share from the heart without
judgments or attempts to make your feelings fade.
Find solace in those who can acknowledge your
grief as part of your wholeness and your wholeness
as part of them. When we honor the grief that
change brings with it, endeavoring to work through
its many layers of sadness – absent of fear, beyond
the need to control – only then will we grow into
our humanity from a place that is truly whole.

Kristen Spexarth

February 12, 2002
Seattle, Washington

Appendix 2: Overview

Passing Reflections is a book that explores the terrain of traumatic loss. While mostly poems, it is in fact a story, a chronological account of my journey through the hours, days and months following the loss of my eldest son, Colby, to suicide. He was twenty-two. My intention in sharing this work is to reach out to others suffering loss and also to reach out to those who would serve them. I often found a void of understanding separating these groups. My aspiration is to help bridge the gap.

I know that when in need it can be difficult to find genuine help. Sometimes people hesitate to reach out because they cannot bear to witness another's pain. And, too, it can be hard to connect with survivors of traumatic loss. Trauma undermines the foundations of one's being—the ground gives way, time stops, we cease to exist as once we did, almost as if there was no one there to reach. When Colby died I felt profoundly alienated from everyone and everything, even from loving family and friends who were trying to help me, and even as I had a pressing need to connect with them in a meaningful way. I found myself inhabiting a parallel world, isolated in the midst of other's normalcy. It can be frightening to find oneself utterly transformed and apparently alone in a strange but vital, new reality.

The stress of being unable to communicate what was real for me set in motion the writing of this book. I desperately needed to connect with others and failing miserably in most of my attempts, fell back on the written word. Deep in shock, at first the writing was simply witnessing; documenting where I was and what was happening inside of me. Later, as I experienced awkward and sometimes hurtful interactions with friends and caregivers, I wrote, trying to help people understand what it is to grieve traumatic loss.

The valuable insights by Elizabeth Kubler-Ross and others into its process, gave us an understanding of the stages of grief. While helping elucidate the fact that grief moves through shock, confusion, guilt, anger and eventually forgiveness and compassion, this process is sometimes misread as a linear progression, a road that starts at one place and ends up in another. I found the stages of grief to be more circular or spiral than linear, always revisiting the beginning, but in a whole new way. Eventually, as I went round and round, I learned to not fear the sudden seismic waves of sadness and guilt that seemed to come out of nowhere. I learned to ride them out. They passed, and at each pass I grew better able to open to, and face what was.

It is hard to watch someone you care for suffer, whether from physical or emotional pain. And how do we separate those anyway, the physical from the mental? Wanting to help us "get over it" is such a natural human response. But traumatized by loss, our bodies, hearts and minds undergo physiological and mental processes that are of vital importance to our well-being. There is no right or wrong way to grieve and healing takes time, sometimes years. Even so, it often seems that almost everyone wants grief to just go away. In an effort to help, family members, friends and caregivers can cause further trauma attempting to "fix" what is "wrong."

The loving intention to help when coming from an urgent need to eradicate pain sometimes goes awry: first, in the aversion to feeling any pain and second, in the refusal to acknowledge that there might, in fact, be some benefit to experiencing pain. My understanding now is that there is no "getting over it." Instead, recovery is a process where we learn to incorporate the pain of loss into the fabric of our lives. This takes time and help from those who can listen without the overlay of their hopes and fears, in other words, without judgments. In time pain softens but it does not go away.

Sometimes I felt a need in others for me to be anywhere but where I was. So great was this pressure that I tried to document my reality, to show the futility of trying to make someone other than what they are. Besides being impossible, it is not helpful. Tears are an interesting case in point. The cultural need to edit our feelings so others will not be uncomfortable is hard on those who grieve. And so I wrote, trying to help people see that if they truly wanted to be supportive, simply listening to, or just sitting quietly and being with me without the need to do or change anything would be the greatest kindness. Bottled tears do not make a good brew. Eventually, unwept grief sours and becomes even harder to bear. And then there were times when I experienced joy and laughter and I was stricken by the thought, "How could I feel joy when he is dead?" And so I wrote, noting that as grief moves we often travel the full range of emotions.

Not only was I surprised by changes in me, but I also learned a great deal about those around me. Many family members and friends and even strangers offered their heartfelt support, while others, even some I thought would, did not. Not everyone can engage the pain of loss. I am grateful to all those who were able to be with me in pain; they helped me to survive. Finding a grief group or counselor who will sit with you and genuinely listen is especially important since it is so difficult for others to approach our pain.

In my search for help after Colby died I saw several counselors. Early on, one of them said, "Never let anyone tell you that you are doing it wrong." Eventually we find a path through loss, sometimes in awkward and uncomfortable ways, but all paths are correct. I derived the greatest benefit from the grief group called Survivors of Suicide (SOS) sponsored by the King County Crisis Clinic in Seattle, Washington, where I had the chance to speak my truth and listen to others suffering loss do the same. I was also fortunate to find and join a spiritual community that has helped me in my healing.

Forgiveness of those who seem to have let us down comes as we gain perspective. Every one of us is doing the best she or he can, including those who suicide, including those so locked inside their judgments they cannot extend. If we could do it differently we would be doing so. Letting go of judgments begins when our hearts are broken open and we understand that there is fundamentally no difference between us, and ultimately nothing missing from what is. At that moment, instead of being frightened by and turning away from hardship or joy, we become able to embrace both and offer each other a helping hand.

Losing my son changed my whole orientation to living. I realized if I was to survive I needed to reach out to others. I am neither a therapist nor do I imagine the poems will be a prescription for all. I simply offer this work to you, hoping you will find in it threads of correspondence, for that is where healing begins.

A Personal Perspective on Resources for Survivors

I've learned many lessons since Colby died, some of which are:

- *To notice sensations/feelings as they manifest in my body*
- *To drop the story line I associate with sensations/feelings and simply notice what is*
- *To acknowledge sensations/feelings by sitting with them, letting them be, and then letting them go*
- *To remember even difficult sensations/feelings eventually pass*
- *To go out into nature when thoughts are lost in tape loops*
- *To seek help when despair moves in*
- *To give myself time alone, to rest and heal*
- *To remember to always bring awareness back to my breath*
- *To quiet my mind through sitting practice*
- *To be kind to myself and others*
- *And in gratitude, to give back when I can*

While this short list might seem easy to note, it has taken me years and much practice to take these simple lessons to heart. The resources that have helped most in this on-going process are described below.

Before Colby died, my life was predicated on the notion that one can control events through the power of one's will. I had been so busy managing things there was little time left for quietude or noticing.

Meaning came via doing and value was measured by deeds accomplished and goods accumulated. With his death, all of that was ripped away.

I remember in the first days saying to those closest to me, "I don't know how to do this!" Hoping to help, friends and family brought me numerous books but I had no patience for them—making no mention of the energies that were coursing through my body rendering me immobile, no mention of the altered state I found myself in where a veil seemed to separate me from everyone—those "how to" books were useless at the beginning. What I most needed from others was wisdom, and at the very least, direct experience.

Conventional wisdom teaches us to turn away from the pain of loss, but somehow I knew that my best chance for survival was to be with what was happening and to explore every sensation, no matter how seemingly dark. Alarmed by the intensity of my grief, some people suggested I get a sedative to alleviate my suffering. They did not realize that, while difficult, being awake and present to my new reality was of vital importance. What I was experiencing was more dynamic and real than anything I had ever known. Forestalling my difficulty was no more an option than was stopping breathing.

For most of my life I've held a Buddhist leaning worldview and there were several Buddhist texts among my books. Wanting to help my son in his transition from this life to the next, I read The Tibetan Book of the Dead: The Great Liberation Through Hearing

In The Bardo, by Francesca Fremantle and Chögyam Trungpa (Shambala, 1975). Whatever benefit that practice may have held for him, reading those verses again and again was a great help to me. Still, many of the images were troubling, so I was grateful to find Sogyal Rinpoche's The Tibetan Book of Living and Dying (Harper Collins, 1992) that guided me through the metaphorical imagery of the teachings on the Bardo.

Six months in, I started attending Survivors of Suicide (SOS) at King County Crisis Clinic. In this twice monthly drop-in support group, I was able to find some peace. But even with this significant aid, I found myself in real trouble emotionally. I realized that if I was going to survive, support of a different kind was needed — inside of me were energies like wild horses, tearing me apart. After running the second red light in a row, it dawned on me, if I did not get my butt on a meditation mat — I might not make it. I searched for and found a Buddhist sangha, a spiritual community. In that setting I was welcomed no matter how broken and was able to broaden my study and practice, attend lectures and retreats where living masters helped me begin to assimilate the teachings.

Besides the two books on the Bardo that anchored me in the very beginning, the following books were pivotal in my search for wisdom and understanding. I list them here in the order I discovered them:

Kay Redfield Jamison, *Night Falls Fast-Understanding Suicide* (Vintage, 2000)

Iris Bolton, *My Son…My Son…* (Bolton Press, 1996)

Judith Lief, *Making Friends With Death: A Buddhist Guide to Encountering Mortality* (Shambala, 2001)

Pema Chödrön, *The Wisdom of No Escape* (Shambala, 1991)

Miriam Greenspan, *Healing through the Dark Emotions: The wisdom of grief, fear, and despair* (Shambala, 2003)

Francesca Fremantle, *Luminous Emptiness* (Shambala, 2001)

Byron Katie, *Loving What Is* (Random House, 2002)

Jon Kabat-Zinn, *Wherever You Go There You Are* (Hyperion, 1994)

Eckhart Tolle, *The Power of Now* (New World Library, 1999)

During all this time, writing was my greatest helper and so I wrote, continuously. The journal form of *Passing Reflections* gives an indication of the flow of this work, slowing as the second year passed. I look back now, eight years later, and can only dimly recall the intensity experienced while writing these poems. The pain of loss has indeed softened, though I do not expect it will ever "go away."

If you are suffering loss, I wish for you wisdom teachings and genuine helpers when you most need them, no matter from which traditions or practices you seek guidance.

Professional Resources for Survivors of Suicide

The following websites have extensive resources dedicated to survivors of traumatic loss.

American Association of Suicidology (AAS)
www.suicidology.org

American Foundation for Suicide Prevention (AFSP)
www.afsp.org

Compassionate Friends
Grief support after the death of a child
www.compassionatefriends.com

Four Seasons Oasis, Seattle, WA
A bookstore with "...resources to maneuver the changes faced while integrating the death of a loved one, the response to a disaster or the effects of an illness."
www.fourseasonsoasis.com

King County Crisis Clinic (KCCC)
Office in Seattle, Washington
www.crisisclinic.org

KCCC Survivor link
Bi-monthly survivor of suicide drop-in clinic in Seattle
www.crisisclinic.org/about3.html

Suicide Prevention Action Network (SPAN)
SPAN is dedicated to preventing suicide through public education and awareness, community action and federal, state and local grassroots advocacy.
www.spanusa.org

Youth Suicide Prevention Program (YSPP)
"Suicide is not chosen; it happens when pain exceeds resources for coping with pain."
www.yspp.org

Index

About the Author

Born in Dayton, Ohio, with early childhood summers spent exploring the shores of Elk Lake in Michigan, Kristen was transplanted to Mercer Island, Washington, when she was eleven. Always drawn to the outdoors and water, she spent her youth enjoying the liquid beauty of the Northwest and then Japan as an exchange student. Her year abroad gave direction to her college studies, starting at the University of Chicago and, after a several-year hiatus working on Cape Cod as a waitress and in upstate New York as an art teacher, she graduated with a BA from Vassar College and an MA from the University of California, at Berkeley (UCB) in Asian Studies.

Settling in El Cerrito, California, she did volunteer work in the community, concentrating on raising a family until both her children were in grade school. Then, realizing she wanted a career in horticulture, she resumed her studies in the community college system. Starting with landscape design and installation, she broadened her working experience at the organic vegetable and native plant gardens of Mudd's Restaurant/Crow Canyon Gardens in San Ramon, California. Another shift in focus to estate gardening brought her to UCB's Blake Garden in Kensington, California, and then back to the Northwest where she has continued to work as a gardener in the public sector.

Her desire to find self-expression through the written word began during her year in Japan in 1965. Coupling the will to write with the inspired instruction of her freshman English teacher at the University of Chicago, the poet Henry Rago, her love of writing as craft began in earnest. Throughout the years of raising a family and learning a trade, Kristen continued to write, tracking her life's journey through dream diaries and journaling. With her eldest son's traumatic death, the foundations of her life were torn away and writing was all that was left. Events following Colby's suicide taught her that she needed to reach out to others who were grieving, and thus *Passing Reflections* was born.